Happy Birthday Steve
don't get better than this.
Big boys toys

Jeff Sill

CW00411202

BIG CAT DIARY

The Last Year of the Jaguar with 6 Squadron RAF

by Wing Commander John Sullivan MBE MSc RAF

*This book is respectfully dedicated
to all 6 Squadron personnel
– past, present and future.*

Acknowledgements

I must thank Karl Drage for giving me the idea to produce this book and for spending so many hours helping me to turn the idea into reality. Rich Cooper was instrumental in making the project viable and James Lawrence brought it all together with indispensable professional expertise and, like Karl, an unwavering enthusiasm. Peter Gallagher, at Ian Allan Printing, had the last crank of the handle. Finally, my thanks to all of the photographers that have contributed their excellent pictures and have supported the Jaguar with such enthusiasm and loyalty for many years.

Big Cat Diary: The Last Year of the Jaguar with 6 Squadron RAF
© John M. Sullivan, 2007

ISBN 978 0 9557247 0 1

Design & Layout
© James Lawrence, Gingercake Creative

Published by John M. Sullivan

Printed in England by
Ian Allan Printing Ltd
Riverdene Business Park, Molesey Road,
Hersham, Surrey KT12 4RG

Front cover: Jamie Hunter
Back cover and title page: Karl Drage

Contents

Foreword

This book was conceived as a personal gift by me, the last Commanding Officer of an RAF Jaguar Squadron, to the personnel of the Squadron as a record, primarily through pictures, of their achievements in the final year of the Jaguar's service. As I began to compile the book, it quickly became apparent that the volume of material demanded a full print run if I was to end up with a book that met my expectations and I have therefore been able to make it more widely available than I originally envisaged. This then, is a personal perspective of the closing of a chapter in RAF history; the retirement from service of the Jaguar after 33 years of stalwart performance on the front-line of the RAF as a ground attack fighter. Though not blessed with classically graceful lines, the Jaguar is nevertheless a very photogenic aeroplane, with a complementary blend of business like angles and shapely curves. The Jaguar was never more at home than when flying fast and low, and most of the images in this book were donated by the legions of Aviation Enthusiasts who had ample opportunity to capture her; I am grateful for their consistent support.

In terms of raw performance, the Jaguar can compete with few other fighters, but she was nevertheless extremely popular among the pilots, or least among those that mastered her, as she could reliably deliver impressive results in her role when handled well. To achieve this though, the pilot had to work hard and be on top of his game and it is not hard to see how a difficult job done well gives rise to immediate satisfaction. The engineers also earned their sense of achievement, constantly putting unserviceable aircraft back into action through the application of experience and their core trade skills, and without a diagnostic programme in sight! In a working environment where general satisfaction reigned, it is not too difficult to see how every other trade, from administration through life support to ops and mission support, also had pride in the contribution that each made to a winning team. Mutual respect is essential, and I personally think that the Jaguar Force was long a happy outfit for the universal understanding that each element of the team had a vital role to play.

In preference to a Mission Statement (I don't think anyone remembers them or considers them on a routine basis) I asked the Jaguar Force to hold one simple maxim in mind when performing their many and varied duties over the last year: Jaguar Force Excellence. I consider that professional excellence was synonymous with the Jaguar Force and, as we approached the end, I wanted to safeguard, and even enhance, that reputation and I wanted every member of the Force to understand, and be proud of, his or her personal contribution. The photographs within celebrate the Jaguar but the book is dedicated to the men and women with whom I served and who rose magnificently above all challenges to give the Jaguar a fitting send off.

I am immensely proud to have been afforded the opportunity to lead the Jaguar Force to its glorious end. I have long pondered the fabled 'Jaguar Spirit' and wondered as to its constituent elements; my personal view is that it was a combination of ethos, defined as 'the distinctive spirit of a people' and élan, an 'enthusiastic and assured vigour and liveliness'. History shows that such qualities are often inculcated in select cadres of individuals, where inclusion must be earned through trial and the gaining of mutual respect.

If the 'Jaguar Spirit' was the distinctive and enthusiastic spirit of a small, select band with assured vigour, then I am proud to have been, and will always consider myself to be, a 'Jag Mate'.

John Sullivan

Wing Commander John Sullivan MBE MSc RAF

Words of Wisdom from the Squadron Warrant Officer

To say the last 18 months of Jaguar service have been a roller coaster ride would be an understatement of monstrous proportion. Move to a new Main Operating Base, commence flying 3 days after arrival, complete 7 detachments around the world and close the Squadron given some six weeks notice and then you might have a feel for just what has been achieved. It has been completed in a safe, timely and utterly professional manner thanks to the efforts of each and every Squadron member. A band of brothers (and to be politically correct, sisters) whose loyalty, dedication and sheer hard work embrace all that is, and has been, Jaguar throughout its many years of service. It is a shame that the Jaguar was retired early and a greater shame that the record of continuous service was stolen from the longest serving Squadron in the world. What can never be taken are the memories and the excellence of the Jaguar Force. Like the Boss and all those who have served on the Jaguar for many years, I am proud to have been associated with the aircraft and the truly awesome people I have met along the way.

Aye, McIntyre

Royal Air Force Coningsby - A New Lair

Royal Air Force Coltishall, the UK home of the Jaguar since 1974, closed on 1 April 2006 and 6 Squadron became the last remaining RAF squadron to operate the Jaguar, commencing operations from RAF Coningsby. 6 Squadron had the honour of leading a Diamond 9 flypast over the ranks of RAF Coltishall as they marched off from the parade ground for the very last time.

The following week saw the Squadron standing up at Coningsby. With the closure of RAF Coltishall, 6 Squadron grew in size, with both pilots and engineers being augmented by personnel from 41 (F) Squadron and other RAF Coltishall units. Despite the turbulence associated with moving 20 Jaguars, some 230 personnel and all of their equipment to a new home, imminent commitments meant that it was important to resume training quickly. The Jaguar Force was well versed in deploying to new locations, usually many thousands of miles away, and commencing operations; this stood the Squadron in good stead, returning to a full training syllabus and launching 18 sorties a day by Friday 7 April.

The change from operating a line of aircraft, as had been the practice at RAF Coltishall, to operating out of a site of Hardened Aircraft Shelters (HAS) presented new challenges, especially in supervising the engineering practices within a dispersed environment. It was credit to the Squadron's engineers at all levels that they were able to adapt so quickly. Senior NCO leadership was especially worthy of note, as was the manner in which the junior Corporals shouldered the responsibility of the HAS Commander role.

Upon arrival, 6 Squadron was the only operational squadron to be based at RAF Coningsby, and the station had become accustomed to very few sorties each day and rarely more than two or three at once. It was therefore a rather rude awakening when 6 Squadron arrived; the Squadron immediately stamped the Jaguar mark on Coningsby, launching a 10-ship formation on a tactical training mission at the end of the first week; the Jaguar Force had arrived!

Inset: **Goodbye Colt.** RAF Coltishall was the last Battle of Britain airfield to host combat aircraft.

Above & Right: **Public Tribute.** Royal Air Force Coltishall enjoyed an excellent rapport with the local community, as evidenced by the strong turnout by locals on 1 April. Their ranks were swollen by many of the stalwart supporters of the Jaguar, many of whom traveled from afar to mark the sad occasion of the base closure. *Andrew Leonard*

Above: **First Foray.** Wing Commander Sullivan was promulgated in orders as the Officer Commanding 6 Squadron from 0900 on Saturday 1 April and less than 2 hours later was leading 11 Jaguars out of the new lair; there could be no better way of assuming command! *Steve Buckby*

Right: **The Flying Canopeners.** The Squadron was so successful at destroying enemy tanks and vehicles in the North African Campaign of World War II, flying Hurricane IIDs armed with 40 mm cannons, that it earned the nickname 'The Flying Canopeners'. *Damien Burke*

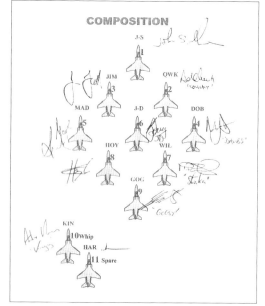

Above: **Diamond 9.** Fittingly, the Diamond 9 comprised 4 established pilots from 6 Squadron, 4 who had just arrived from 41 (F) Squadron and the new 'Boss'. *Damien Burke*

Top: **Coltishall Salute.** *Ian Sayer*

Above: **Ten Jaguars – Break to Land.** Many units reserve Friday afternoons for maintenance. Not so the Jaguar! *Geoff Hibbert*

The Jaguars – An Expeditionary Force

The Jaguar Force was an expeditionary Force, capable of deploying at short notice, standing-up in an austere environment and quickly generating effective combat air power. After arriving at RAF Coningsby, the Squadron had only 2 weeks to bed-in and complete preparations for another major training deployment – 10 aircraft to Thumrait in Oman for Exercise Magic Carpet 06.

Magic Carpet presented an excellent opportunity for the new mix of personnel to bond together into a single team, as 6 Squadron, and proved to be an immensely successful detachment. The engineering effort was superb, achieving a 94% sortie strike rate against a challenging programme of day and night flying that encompassed the most demanding flying disciplines of the Jaguar; dropping live weapons, flying at operational heights of just 100 feet in unusual terrain, and executing night missions by using Night Vision Goggles. These tasks are inherently hazardous, with little margin for error, but the Squadron performed incredibly well, expending the full scale of live weapons

and, most notably, achieving a full house of success in delivering and guiding Laser Guided Bombs (LGBs) onto specially constructed targets.

The results would have been impressive under any circumstances but in the extremely testing conditions that existed in Oman, where temperatures exceeded 50 ºC on the flight line and 65 ºC in the cockpit, they were quite outstanding. The Boss made a point of frequently gathering all of the engineers together to brief them on where the Squadron stood in the Exercise and what was at stake, principally his concern at the lack of any margin for error, given the scale of the task that the Squadron had shouldered in coming out to Oman so soon after relocating to Coningsby. As the engineering achievement unfolded during the exercise, he quickly dubbed the troops 'Wizards'!

Subsequent deployments, in just the last year alone, took the Squadron to Cyprus, Jordan, Scotland, Belgium and the United Arab Emirates.

In Jordan, a nation with which 6 Squadron enjoys particularly strong ties, the

Squadron brought the work hard, play hard ethic to the fore. In just eight productive days of training, the Squadron dropped 10 LGBs and 40 inert 1000 lb free-fall bombs which all struck their targets, and flew Close Air Support Missions (CAS) that trained four new Forward Air Controllers from the British Army, who then deployed to Iraq and Afghanistan. In 17 days the Squadron transported and set up a deployed operating unit, flew 104 sorties with a 92% serviceability rate, visited a clutch of the world's most spectacular sights, such as Wadi Rhum, Petra and the Dead Sea, and all recovered safely to the UK. Hopefully, the Squadron also made a tangible difference to Defence Diplomacy by reinforcing cultural and operational links with a staunch ally in an unstable theatre at a time of increased tension.

The last RAF Jaguar detachment was to the UAE which was, ironically, a new destination for the Jaguar Force. The exercise provided training alongside French, US and Saudi forces, as well as those of the host nation.

Above: **Getting There.** Successfully deploying up to 10 aircraft to an unfamiliar base many thousands of miles away is a major undertaking in its own right. Without an autopilot, the Jaguar pilot must remain alert and fly the aircraft manually at all times. A perk of the job is always getting a window seat!

Above: **Heavy Support.** The Air Transport (AT) Fleet of the RAF provides the horsepower to get the rest of the team into position. This C17 of 99 Squadron took the bulk of 6 Squadron personnel to the UAE, with the advance party traveling by the far less comfortable C130.

Above: **First Class Travel.** After driving through the night to RAF Brize Norton, the team catch some rest in the hold of the C17, in among essential stores and equipment. Most major deployments will also require a sea move of spares and heavy equipment. *All images Mark Discombe*

Top Left: **Along for the Ride.** When the 2-seat trainers (the 'T-birds') are deployed, the opportunity arises to take a passenger. Here, Sqn Ldr Mark Hodge, the Senior Engineering Officer or SEngO, tells Flt Lt Liz Shaw, the Junior Engineering Officer, of his wonder at having survived 3 consecutive sorties in an aeroplane that has been subject to pilot maintenance only! *Jim Burden*

Above: **Walking the Line.** Back in a more familiar role, SEngO surveys the scene in the lull before the mayhem of the day commences. *Jim Burden*

Far Left: **KFF.** Sergeant Doris Day prepares free-fall 1000 lb bombs (KFF) for loading. *Derek Bower*

Left: **LGB Load Out.** A 1000 lb LGB is loaded for flight. *Derek Bower*

Above: **Getting the Point.** Dick Hodgson gives direction in Line Control.
Jim Burden

Top Right: **Signing Out.** Disco and TC check the aircraft documentation before
'walking' for their sortie, under the watchful eye of Wraggy. *Mark Hodge*

Right: **Pilots Walking.** JT walks out for a sortie on Exercise Magic Carpet in
Oman. Frankie and Kev are ahead. *Jim Burden*

Far Right: **Pax Flight.** Deployments often present the opportunity to fly the
groundcrew in the T-birds, giving them better insight to what training sorties
routinely entail. Tudor prepares to fly with the QWI, Matt 'Petley' Peterson.
Jim Burden

Above: **Desert Teamwork.** Baggy carries out a last quick check before EQ taxys. *Derek Bower*

Right: **Another Passenger.** Melv assists his fellow technician, Craig Jordan, to strap-in. *Jim Burden*

Far Right: **Nervous?** Coggers is clearly delighted at the prospect of another unsuspecting victim! *Jim Burden*

(For the record - Craig had a great trip!)

Above Images: **Sand.** The fine desert sand can quickly get into the cockpit, covering everything. *All images Jim Burden*

Left: **Last Check.** The Line Walker also casts his experienced eye over each aircraft as they head for the runway, alert to anything that might be amiss.

Top Left: **Desert Cat.** On the ORP at Azraq.
Derek Bower

Above: **Line Up.** A pair backtrack then turn around, making use of the entire runway length. EY carrying 2 x KFFs. *Derek Bower*

Middle Left: **Desert Duck!** ED 'the Duck' takes the runway. *Derek Bower*

Far Left: **LGB.** EU approaches the runway with a centreline Paveway II LGB. *Derek Bower*

Left: **Hold Short.** Waiting in turn for an RJAF F16 to take-off. *Derek Bower*

Right: **4-Ship Line-Up.** Forming up for a stream departure. *Derek Bower*

Above: **Desert Duties.** EB high over the Jordanian desert. *Derek Bower*

Top Right & Right: **Desert Cousins.** Omani Jaguars practice refuelling from an RAF VC10, demonstrating the value of mutual training. *Jim Burden*

Left: **CAS Pair.** EB dispenses a flare while on the wing of EZ. Flares are dispensed manually so the pilot must remain alert and practice searching for incoming missiles. *Derek Bower*

Above Left: **Desert Strip.** The view on the approach to Azraq. *Derek Bower*

Left: **Landing Flare.** With the airbrakes out and the tailplane digging in to kill as much speed as possible, EH prepares for touchdown. *Derek Bower*

Above: **Stores Gone.** The protruding rams of the centreline station reveal that EG has successfully dropped its weapon. *Derek Bower*

Right: **Brakes On.** JFE makes its debut in the UAE! *Jim Burden*

Top: **Post Flight Line.** *Jim Burden*

Above: **Hot Stuff.** Having escaped the sweltering confines of the cockpit, Jimmy, Matt and Disco stroll in from a sortie. *Derek Bower*

Right: **Jaguar Tails.** *Derek Bower*

Top Left: **Under Cover.** Rectification work is conducted under shade if at all possible. *Jim Burden*

Middle Left: **Local Sights.** A reminder of the local geography. *Derek Bower*

Bottom Left: **No Hiding.** Richie admires SEngO's new, portable light set – ideal for keeping an eye on proceedings after dark! *Jim Burden*

Above: **Desert Graveyard.** A sad reminder of the looming end date for the Jag. *Derek Bower*

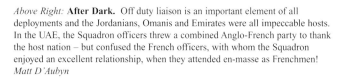

Above & Left: **Desert Sunset.** A GR stands ready, loaded with another LGB, for the next mission. *Jim Burden*

Above Right: **After Dark.** Off duty liaison is an important element of all deployments and the Jordanians, Omanis and Emirates were all impeccable hosts. In the UAE, the Squadron officers threw a combined Anglo-French party to thank the host nation – but confused the French officers, with whom the Squadron enjoyed an excellent relationship, when they attended en-masse as Frenchmen! *Matt D'Aubyn*

Right: **Roses Among Thorns.** Liz Shaw (JEngess), Hannah French (OpsO) and Rachel Clarke (IntO) swap combat uniforms for more glamorous attire to attend the formal dinner that the Squadron traditionally held during each detachment. Tragically, Rachel, always so full of life, was killed in a car accident just a few weeks after the Squadron disbanded. *Mark Discombe*

Above: **Homebound.** Somewhere over the Middle East while RTB UK. *John Sullivan*

Right: **En Route.** In the absence of ground engineering support, the pilot must complete essential maintenance tasks before and after each flight. Here, despite the 'helpful advice' from Bob and the Boss, Rob has finally given up trying to fasten the notoriously fiddly oil inspection panel and steps aside to watch a master – Disco! *Matt D'Aubyn*

Below: **Two's Company.** Like operations, all transits are flown as a pair as a minimum, for mutual support. *John Sullivan*

UK Training

Without the need to continually train new pilots, the Squadron seized an opportunity to 'raise the bar'; increasingly complex training missions took advantage of the Jaguar's sophisticated Helmet Mounted Sight and data-link to develop further the skills of the pilots. All training was designed to ensure relevance to the ongoing operational environments as well as developing skills that would be valuable and transferable to future appointments.

Below: **The Canopeners.** 6 Squadron personnel, assembled in front of HAS 8 in the summer of 2006. *Babbs Robinson/Scott Lewis*

Above: **Cold Start.** A pair of GRs silently await the groundcrew who will prepare them for flight. *Richard Cooper*

Above: **Jaguar Cockpit.** Over the years, additional equipment has been crammed into the Jaguar cockpit, bringing increased weapon delivery accuracy and new capabilities. The result is a messy but comfortably familiar layout. *Karl Drage*

Above Right: **Walkround.** Smithy, the XO for the last few months, completes his pre-flight external checks. *Karl Drage*

Right: **Wet Cat.** Rain pouring into an open cockpit can often not be avoided but it rarely bodes well; you wouldn't pour water over your desktop PC! *Karl Drage*

Left: **UK Ops.** Chris Hoyle and Jim Luke plan a training sortie in the UK. *Karl Drage*

Above: **Jag Dance.** The Liney confirms control surface movement to the pilot. *Karl Drage*

Right: **Emerging from the Lair.** Rob Leather taxys from HAS 8. *Karl Drage*

Top Left: **See you later.** JD cannot hide his pleasure. *Karl Drage*

Above Left: **Time to reflect.** After the inevitable planning frenzy and the barrage of information during the sortie brief, the 7 minute taxy out to the runway provides a welcome opportunity to contemplate the demands of the impending sortie. *Paul Dunn*

Left: **Take-Off.** With a chop of the leader's hand, both aircraft release their brakes. Burners are engaged upon his head nod. *Stephen Boreham*

Above: **Pair + Bounce.** A pair prepare to depart for a Simulated Attack Profile (SAP). Their mission will be opposed by the no. 3 Jaguar who will simulate an enemy aircraft and harass them, attempting to achieve a simulated kill or deny them a successful attack. *Richard Cooper*

Opposite: **Pairs Take-Off.** Aircraft take off in pairs to cut down on comms with ATC and to keep the formation together while negotiating cloud en route to the target area. *Karl Drage*

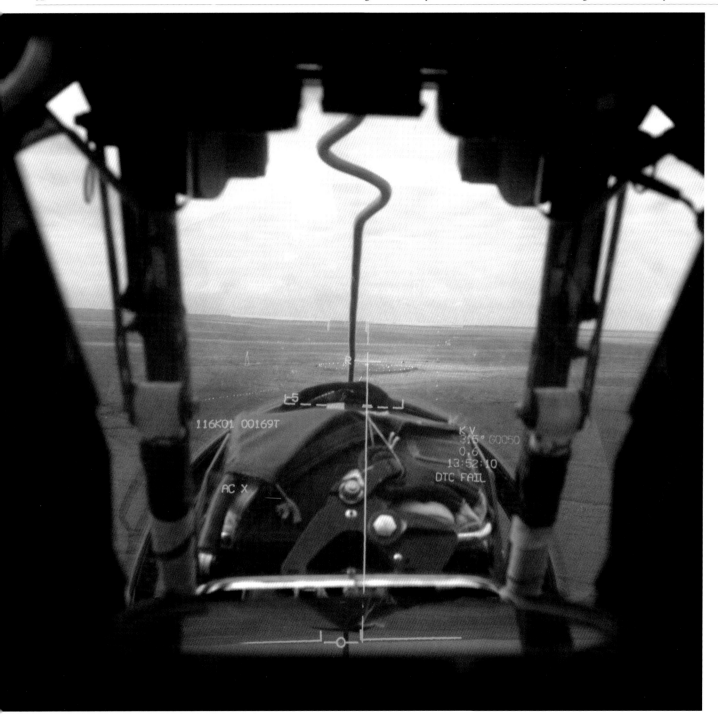

Top: **In Hot.** A GR runs in to target on Donna Nook Air Weapon Range.
Robert Hardy

Left: **Late Arm.** Running in at 150 feet and 450 knots, the pilot lines-up the aircraft with the target, makes the Late Arm 'Live' and 'Commits' the attack.
Gary Morgan

Above: **Off Hot.** A 3Kg practice bomb, which simulates the ballistic path of the larger and more destructive 1000 lb retarded bomb (KRet), is released on target.
Robert Hardy

This Page: **Dive Recovery.** Vapour trails often form at the wing tips when g is pulled, such as during this dive recovery *Richard Cooper/Jamie Hunter*

Above: **Committal.** Jaguar pilots must develop an instinct for how hard they can manoeuvre their platform at low-level. Nose position is critical as too nose-low an attitude can quickly exceed the ability of the aircraft to avoid the terrain, especially in mountainous areas. This GR has committed itself to a route between the surrounding high ground. *Richard Cooper*

Above: **Silhouette.** Dramatic contrast against a stormy sky. *Richard Cooper*

This Page: **Camouflage.** The low-visibility camouflage is effective against a variety of backgrounds. *Richard Cooper*

Above: **Tempest 2.** Jaguar T4 low level through a Welsh valley.
Phil Stevens

Right: **OLF.** Operational Low Flying at 100 feet in the Moffat Valley.
Mark McGrath

Far Right: **Clean.** A GR in a 'clean' configuration, carrying no stores.
Richard Cooper

Left: **Up Close.** A clean GR in the Machynlleth Loop in LFA 7, Wales.
Karl Drage

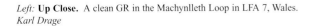

Above: **Overbank.** This GR overbanks aggressively to follow the contours of the terrain closely. 'Ballooning' high increases exposure to threats. *Karl Drage*

Left: **Mach Loop.** A T-bird half way around the Mach Loop. *Karl Drage*

Right: **Rockin' at Low Level.** A T4 manoeuvres aggressively, condensing water from the atmosphere in the partial vacuum that the high wing loading creates. *Barry Price*

Above: **The Wingman's Nightmare!** Trying to formate on a leader who has gone straight into sun. The GR is carrying 2 x KRets on the centerline station. *Ian Black*

Left: **Vertical Pair.** Standard training fit with a centreline CBLS. *Jamie Hunter*

Above: **Approach to Land.** Unrefuelled, training sorties typically last about 1½ hours. *Karl Drage*

Right: **Lossie Touchdown.** Landing at RAF Lossiemouth on the last Jaguar landaway. *Jason Grant*

Above: **Taxy Back.** Returning to Echo HAS site with brake 'chutes deployed. *Karl Drage*

Left: **Brakes On.** Daubs acknowledges the Liney's instruction to apply the brakes. *Karl Drage*

Right: **And Relax.** A welcome blast of cool air as the canopy is raised at the end of a hard working sortie. *Karl Drage*

Far Right : **Turnround After Flight.** Check of the front end of the No. 2 engine as the jet is prepared for the next sortie while 'Rigger' Blakey inspects the reheat module of the No. 1 engine. *Both Karl Drage*

Above: **Ready for Bed.** Pinned and chocked, this T4 is ready for push back into its HAS. *Karl Drage*

Far Left: **Aden.** The business end of the Aden 30 mm cannon. *Al MacNeish*

Left: **Vapour Gutters.** Close up of the reheat module. *Alex Turtle*

Right: **Night Cat.** The Jaguar Force was fully night capable. Night Vision Goggles (NVGs) allow the pilot to see in the dark, while advanced targeting sensors, like the TIALD pod on the starboard wing, can detect the Infra-Red emissions and guide an LGB (port wing) to their target. *Dr Séan Wilson*

Big 6

On Tuesday 24 April 2007, the Boss announced to the Squadron that the Jaguar Out of Service Date was to be brought forward to Monday 30 April 2007. All operationally orientated training would cease on that date and the Jaguar would no longer be a deployable Force Element. Delivery of the airframes to Cosford would then commence and any ceremonial flying had to be concluded during May.

Naturally, this came as a great disappointment to all members of the Jaguar Force. It was not considered feasible to organise an event to celebrate 33 years of stalwart service with due gravity with only 5 weeks notice. Such short notice would also compromise attendance. The end of May was therefore chosen for a Squadron Disbandment Parade but the weekend of 29 June – 1 July 2007 was selected for the final Jaguar Farewell, reluctantly accepting that this would be without the nostalgia of RAF Jaguar flying.

In the meantime though, the Squadron resolved to go in style, and spun up for one last land away to Lossiemouth in Scotland, the very next day.

Despite ongoing tasking all over the UK, 10 Jaguars all converged on Lossie at the end of the day! Returning on the Thursday, the Boss decided to replicate the famous 6 Squadron 'Big 6' formation, flown by Venoms in the 1950s. He outlined his plan to achieve this on the last day of declared operational service, with a practice on Friday 27 April to mitigate against poor weather or aircraft unserviceability. This was a challenging formation to fly, and not without the risk inherent in any unusual venture, especially those that include 12 jets in close proximity! The endeavour was therefore briefed exceptionally carefully, and the pilots walked through the entire routine a number of times in the car park. The practice went well but was limited to just 12 available pilots and so had to dispense with the luxury of an airborne spare and whip. Even so, the engineers put 14 aircraft on the line; given that one of the 15 was in the paint shop and the Squadron had just recovered from a gruelling overseas detachment, this was little short of magic – fully justifying the tongue in cheek nickname the Boss reserved for the 6 Squadron engineers – 'the Wizards'!

On Monday 30 April, the weather gods were kind, rewarding the Squadron with a brilliant blue sky. With 13 pilots available and thanks again to the Wizards, the venture had the luxury of an airborne spare who could also act as whip. The practice had gone extremely well but, as is their habit, the pilots analysed their performance critically to determine where improvements could be made. The formation references were adjusted slightly to produce a tighter formation, conscious, of course, of the need to remain safe. Adjustments were also made to the line that the formation would fly across RAF Coningsby; by flying along the southern taxy-way, and thus over the popular spotter sites at each end of the airfield, rather than directly along the runway and therefore oblique to most of the popular locations, it was hoped that the assembled crowds would be afforded a better angle on the formation. The formation was flown to great effect, marking a sad occasion with pride and professional excellence!

Kneeboard guide to who, what and when!

Formation Line-Up.

Idiot's Guide to a 'Big 6' and 12-Ship Opposition Breaks for Dummies!

Above: **Whatever.** The news of the Squadron's early closure is met with indifference! *Karl Drage*

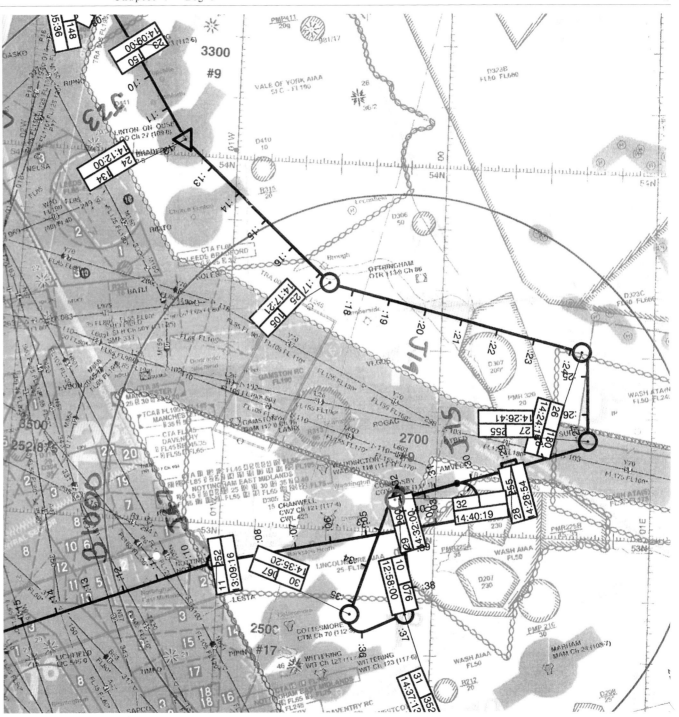

Right: Map of the route over eastern England.

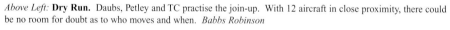

Above Left: **Dry Run.** Daubs, Petley and TC practise the join-up. With 12 aircraft in close proximity, there could be no room for doubt as to who moves and when. *Babbs Robinson*

Above Right: **Big 6.** The Boss commits to memory the sequence of the sortie and the boys 'walk-through' the formation changes. *Babbs Robinson*

Left: **Behind the Scenes.** Amanda and Gemma holding the fort! They were the unsung heroines of the early closure, coping brilliantly with the mountain of administrative tasks that suddenly needed to be addressed. *Babbs Robinson*

Far Left: **Line Control.** Sgt Al Miller coordinates jets on 30 April 2007. *Babbs Robinson*

Above: **The Game's Afoot.** Thirteen Jaguars taxy out to Runway 07.
Babbs Robinson

Right: **Mass Launch.** JD leads the Back 4 onto the runway after the Front 9 have launched. *Michael Hind*

Above: **JFE.** Jaguar Force Excellence. *Sally Monk*

Left: **UK Tour.** The route on 30 April took in the airfields at RAF Shawbury, RAF Valley, Warton, RAF Leeming, Topcliffe, RAF Linton-on-Ouse and Donna Nook Air Weapon Range before arriving back at RAF Coningsby. *Sally Monk*

Right: **6-Ship?** One minute out from RAF Leeming, ATC asked, 'Confirm you're a 6-ship?' The response: 'Affirm – you'll understand in 60 seconds!' *Sally Monk*

1. Wg Cdr John Sullivan 'BOS'

2. Sqn Ldr Dave Stephen 'STU'

3. Flt Lt Bob Bailey 'BOB'

4. Flt Lt Matt D'Aubyn 'DOB'

5. Flt Lt Matt Peterson 'PET'

6. Flt Lt Chris Hoyle 'HOY'

7. Flt Lt Jim Luke 'LUK'

8. Flt Lt Shane Harrison 'HAR'

9. Flt Lt Tim Clement 'T-C'

11. Flt Lt Rob Leather 'LET'
& Sgt Griff Lay

10. Flt Lt John Davy 'J-D'
& Flt Lt Hannah French 'OPSO'

12. Flt Lt 'Stuka' Wilson 'WIL'

Photograph: Karl Drage

Left: **Perfect 9.** Diamond Formation by the Front 9. *Karl Drage*

Above: **Kite.** Diamond + Four, formed up for the Break. *Karl Drage*

Far Left: **Initials.** Kite settling down in turbulent conditions on the run in to break. *Damien Burke*

Left: **Opposition Break.** Thirteen Jags breaking in opposition to land. *Damien Burke*

Above: **Break, Break, Go!** Symmetry is preserved. *Mark Rouse*

Right: Last 4 of the Diamond. *Martin Keen*

Far Left: **Zipping Together.** The opposition circuits zip together on finals for a coordinated landing sequence. *Damien Burke*

Left: **Short Finals.** *Damien Burke*

Above: **Taxy Back.** *Babbs Robinson*

Right: **Mission Accomplished!** The Boss indicates his approval and acknowledges the strong turnout by Jaguar enthusiasts. *Karl Drage*

Above: **Post Flight Pose.** TC falls victim to Evil Bob. *Babbs Robinson*

2000 Hours Jaguar

In May, the Squadron conducted essential currency flying only and the Boss was therefore fortunate to still be able to achieve the significant milestone of 2000 Jaguar hours. This endeavour was assisted by the unusual number of aircraft that needed a late afternoon flight check! This did, however, present a timely opportunity to get through the majority of the engineers on the passenger list (it always seemed to be the T-birds?) for which they were appreciative – even if they did have to endure a 2-hour sortie to the north-west tip of Scotland and back!

Below Left: **Cracked It!** The Boss taxys in on 23 May 07 after notching up 2000 Jaguar hours. *Karl Drage*

Below: **Cheers!** Stumper, OC B Flt, is thoughtfully on hand with a new Jag Patch and a bottle of champagne. *Karl Drage*

Above: **2000+ Hours.** It is traditional to mark such milestones in the aviating career of a pilot. The team assemble for a formal photograph… *Karl Drage*

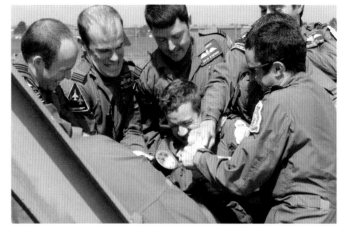

…and then decide that the Boss should not be spared the rest of the traditional treatment!   *Babbs Robinson*

Top Right & Middle: The 'bodge tape' is a wise precaution. *Babbs Robinson*

Right: No fire extinguishers were hurt in the making of this book.
Babbs Robinson

6 Squadron Disbandment Parade

On 31 May 2007, 6 Squadron disbanded for the first time since it had formed on 24 January 1914. The occasion was marked by a parade in which the Squadron handed over its Sovereign Standard for safe custody until the Squadron reforms.

The Squadron drilled hard, determined to do justice to the event, and they wore their pride fiercely when they stood in front of the Chief of the Air Staff, the Reviewing Officer, and their families. On the day, their discipline and determination could not have been more obvious and the parade was executed

flawlessly; the chief concern of the Boss was of letting them down by mixing up the bewildering sequence of orders that the RAF Regiment instructor insisted was 'obvious' and refused to commit to paper! Fortunately, he prevailed.

Above: **Disbandment Parade.** The Chief of the Air Staff, Sir Glenn Torpy, himself a former Jaguar pilot, takes the salute as the Reviewing Officer. *Damien Burke*

Above: **General Salute.** The General Salute is marked by an overflight by Squadron Jaguars in Vixen formation. *Karl Drage*

Left: **Standard Party.** The Squadron's Sovereign Standard is carried onto the parade by the Standard Bearer, Flt Lt Bob Bailey, flanked by the Standard Escorts: Chief Technicians Roy Wilkes and Andy Maginnes and Warrant Officer McIntyre. *Karl Drage*

Top Left: OC 6 Squadron seeks permission to handover the Squadron Standard. *Karl Drage*

Above: **Escorts Take Post.** The Squadron Standard is handed over to Flt Lt Charlie Lynn of the RAF Regiment, symbolically passing into his safe custody until the Squadron is reformed. In practice, the Standard will reside within College Hall Officers' Mess at RAF Cranwell, along with the Royal Jordanian Standard. *Damien Burke*

Right: **General Salute.** The Boss is clearly not happy to relinquish the Standard. *Karl Drage*

Above: **Gulf War Jaguar.** EE, now rebadged T, is repainted in the desert pink camouflage of the 1991 Persian Gulf War and is ready in time to provide a backdrop to the parade. *Karl Drage*

Left: **Gulf War Nose Art.** XX725 served in the 1991 conflict as T; some artistic license was applied to the nose art though. The design, by ex-6 Squadron SNCO, Sgt Mike Richardson, was 'representative' of the non-PC 1990s but much better than the original! *Karl Drage*

Above: **March Off.** The Squadron marches past. *Karl Drage*

Right: **Vixen Break.** Timed to perfection as the Squadron marched past in front of the Reviewing Officer. *Karl Drage*

Far Right: **A Sense of History.** Past – Future – Present. *Karl Drage*

RAF Cosford – Final Resting Place of the Jaguar

All of the Jaguars were destined for RAF Cosford, and, with a runway just 3700 ft long (6000 feet is normally considered uncomfortably short), a 20 ft high railway embankment one end and 60 ft ravine at the opposite end, the Squadron put a lot of thought into getting this done safely. A 'clean' configuration (without external stores) was chosen to permit the lowest possible weight and therefore speed on the approach to land. Similarly, landing would only be attempted when the weather permitted a low diversion fuel into the nearby airfield at RAF Shawbury, and afforded a dry runway, a headwind of at least 10 knots, and no significant cross-wind. All of the brake parachutes were deployed regularly in their last few flights from Coningsby and the rarely used arrestor hooks all exercised to ensure that they operated correctly. The optimum technique for landing was also determined and all nominated pilots practised landing on 'the numbers' and on speed. As each aircraft made its approach, a wingman shadowed him in loose arrow to alert the approach pilot immediately by radio if the chute failed to deploy properly, thus enabling him to immediately prepare for engagement of the specially installed Portable Arrestor Gear, without waiting for chute retardation to be felt and the inevitable and critical delay incurred before realising that it had failed. Airbrakes were selected 'out' once committed to the runway and below single engine overshoot height and it was determined that it was safe to select the chute in the landing flare so that it was fully deployed as the main wheels touched down. The landings were necessarily firm, but testament to the Jaguar's great undercarriage!

The result was that all of the Jaguars landed safely and without incident, without even a single cable engagement.

Above: **Into the Unknown.** The first 5 Jaguars flew into Cosford on 18 May. *Karl Drage*

Above: **Recce Pass.** With a railway line in the undershoot and a ravine in the overshoot, each pilot flew down the runway to assess the hazards. *Jason Grant*

Above: **Low Overshoot.** *Jason Grant*

Above: **Pairs Approach.** Each landing aircraft was shadowed. *Jason Grant*

Right: **Streamed Landing.** ED with chute deployed early. *Jason Grant*

Above: **Rough Field Capability.** The Boss revalidates the Jaguar's capability on poorly prepared or grass strips! *Karl Drage*

Right: **Last Line.** Smartly lined up – probably for the last time. *Karl Drage*

Above: **The First Five.** A senior team was chosen for the first attempt at landing on such a challenging runway: JD, Disco, the Boss, Stumper and Petley. *Kris Thom*

Right: **Goodbye ED 'the Duck'.** Thanks for keeping us safe. *Kris Thom*

Above: **12 June 2007.** The next 8 arrive. *Karl Drage*

Left: **The Delivery Team.** DReg, Evil Bob, Daubs, Jim, Boss, Smithy, Rob, TC and Stuka. *Karl Drage*

Far Left: **Reflecting.** DReg takes a moment to consider his long association with the Jag. DReg made an invaluable contribution in organising many aspects of the Drawdown and earned honorary membership of 6 Squadron – and a place in one of the last flights. *Karl Drage*

Above: **Where Big Cats Go to Die.** After 33 years on the front line, the jets are consigned to ignominious storage. *Karl Drage*

Left: **Signing In.** Jim Luke completes the F700 for the last time. *Karl Drage*

The Painted Cats

The Boss was determined to mark the passing of the Jaguar with a commemorative paint scheme that was somewhat 'different' from the relatively mundane variations of fin and spine that are the usual product of the strict guidelines put forth by the 'camouflage working group'. Conscious that the Jaguar was no longer a deployable element, he reasoned that such restrictions no longer applied; incredibly, approval was received for the very ambitious scheme that was proposed to the appropriate authority – the Squadron was convinced that it must have been signed off by a very busy officer who might not have thoroughly examined what was being proposed!

Nevertheless, that was only the first of many hurdles, which included the need to secure the active support of the RAF Painters and Finishers at a time when they were disappointed to learn that their trade was to be disestablished, the technical challenge of the complex scheme, the costs involved when it became apparent that external assistance was needed, the difficulty in sourcing sponsorship (especially for so little return) as no public money could be used, the untimely unserviceability of the spray bay, and the ever present concern that the venture might be deemed to be drawing too much attention to a 'quiet' departure! The result, however, was worth the effort involved. One aircraft was painted in the 'desert pink' of the 1991 Persian Gulf conflict, arguably the 'Finest Hour' of the Jaguar, complete with 'representative' nose-art. The second

aircraft was designed to represent the skin peeling back from the airframe, under the sustained effect of the slipstream over such an extended period, to reveal the long-suppressed true colours that lay beneath – the Jaguar's spots! This was almost certainly the most ambitious and colourful scheme ever applied to an RAF aircraft.

It is unfortunate that the Squadron was afforded so little opportunity to show them off – they would have made a striking addition to the 2007 airshow circuit and the Queen's Birthday Flypast! Credit for the professional application of these superb schemes, especially within such an extremely challenging timeframe, lies with the RAF Painters and the team from Jaguar Cars.

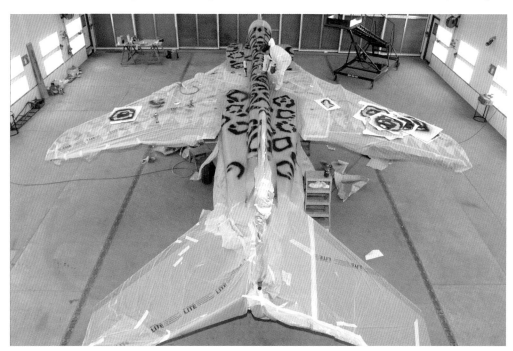

Above: **Work in Progress.** The scheme takes shape amid great secrecy within the paint bay at RAF Coningsby. *Babbs Robinson*

Above: **Finishing Touches.** After applying the last details, 'the Cat' was towed across to the Squadron HAS Site in the dead of night to ensure that its roll out was not compromised by early sightings from outside the wire. *Richard Cooper*

Chapter 8 – The Painted Cats

Above: **Job Done!** The Boss thanks the RAF Coningsby painters when 'the Cat' is first brought out into the daylight for preliminary photos. *Scott Lewis*

Above: **More Wizards!** Sgt Al Vernon and Joe Buck were instrumental in achieving the final design. *Scott Lewis*

Above: **Jaguar Tail.** All former Jaguar Squadrons are proudly represented. *Karl Drage*

Above: **Desert Cat See-Off.** Charlie Rathbone assists Stumper to strap into T. *Karl Drage*

Left: **True Colours.** The 'True Colours' of the Cat are finally revealed! *Karl Drage*

Above: **Jaguar Stack.** EB (rebadged AI), T and EX. *Jamie Hunter*

Left: **Desert Cat, Lincolnshire Wolds** *Richard Cooper*

This Page: **High Flight.** Oh! I have slipped the surly bonds of Earth and danced the skies on laughter-silvered wings. *Jamie Hunter*

Above: **Head On.** *Richard Cooper*

Above: **Closer.** Stumper brings T astern the ramp of a C130. *Richard Cooper*

Above: **Breaking Left.** Up and over the stern of a Hawk, courtesy of 100 Squadron. *Jamie Hunter*

Spot the Jaguar! Thanks to Jaguar Cars. *Jamie Hunter*

And co-sponsors, Aircraft Illustrated. *Richard Cooper*

Above: **Break Out Left.** *Richard Cooper*

Left: **Line Astern.** *Richard Cooper*

Far Left: **Closing Up.** *Richard Cooper*

Right: **Up close and personal.** *Scott Lewis*

This Spread: Sunward I've climbed and joined the tumbling mirth, of sun-split clouds. *Jamie Hunter*

Jaguar Farewell Weekend

The disbandment events were an immense undertaking to organise, compounded by having so little notice and with the distraction of trying to post all 200+ of the Squadron personnel, close the Squadron and make arrangements for the safe delivery of the jets into Cosford. However, the team performed superbly and all of the planned events went off like clockwork. All in all, a fitting end.

Inexplicably, a trail of very large paw prints suddenly appeared within the HAS site, leading from the Sqn building, out and directly over 2 nearby shelters. 11 Squadron, who will inherit the site, were not as pleased – even less so when they first looked down from the circuit and saw the 40 ft Jag Badge on the roof!

Below Left: **Finishing Touches.** Corporal Russ Horton removes the safety pins and makes sure everything is right before the Enthusiasts' Day commences on 29 June 2007. *Richard Cooper*

Bottom Left: **Start Up.** SAC Kevin Wilson on duty as T completes the start up routine. *Richard Cooper*

Below: **Demonstration.** Daubs takes his turn to fire up T, assisted by Rik Hampson. *Richard Cooper*

Above: **Watching Us…** *Jeff Hutson*

Below: **Watching You!** *Jeff Hutson*

Above: **Reflecting.** *Damien Burke*

Right: **Stick Top.** Smithy ambushes the Boss to present him with a Stick Top, a gift from the Squadron officers. *Karl Drage*

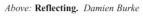

Above: **What Badge?!** *Mark Hodge/Ian Smith*

Left: **Big Cat.** *Karl Drage*

Final Flight

The last 3 Jaguars touched down at RAF Cosford on 2 July 2007. Fittingly, Flt Lt Matt D'Aubyn, the last Jaguar pilot to be trained, was the last to depart from RAF Coningsby. At Cosford the Boss landed last, simply to ensure that his charges were safe on the ground and that he could land knowing that he had discharged the last of his duties.

Right: **Farewell Coningsby.** On 2 July 2007, the last three 6 Squadron Jaguars take-off in stream due to the mismatched fits, the Boss leading, with Sqn Ldr Ian Smith, with SEngO along for the occasion, and then Flt Lt Matt D'Aubyn following at 10 second intervals. *All images Mark Dixon*
Opposite Page: **Last Charge.** AI caught briefly at low level, en route to RAF Cosford. *Richard Cooper*

Main Image: **Shadow.** The Boss escorts Smithy down. *Karl Drage*

Above Left: **Touchdown.** EX lands 'on the numbers'. *Karl Drage*

Left: **Penultimate Landing.** Daubs brings the nosewheel down. *Karl Drage*

Right: **Good Chute.** No problem! *Karl Drage*

Above: **Final Team.** Boss, Smithy, Daubs and SEngO. *Karl Drage*

Right: **Last Goodbyes.** *Karl Drage*

Far Right: **JFE!** *Damien Burke*

Above: **Still Time for Banter.** The Boss rubs salt in the wound, presenting the badge of Smithy's future! The lift awaits. *Karl Drage*

Left: **End of the Line.** End of the Line. All of the RAF Squadrons to have flown the Jaguar were represented on the Final Flight. The responsibility of being the last guardian of the Jaguar Force spirit and reputation was not lost upon the Boss. *Karl Drage*

Above: **Sleeping Now.** *Karl Drage*

Postscript – Jaguar Force Excellence

When I arrived, I was determined that the Squadron would remain operationally viable to the end. In the UAE, our last deployment, I saw enough to convince me that 6 Squadron personnel had exceeded my high expectations and were the very epitome of 'excellence'.

I have also contemplated the Jaguar's contribution to the history of the RAF. It was a mainstay of the frontline in the Cold War and has been on the ramparts for over 33 years in all and yet, as it retires, the dangers are ever present: I decided that I could not improve upon Rudyard Kipling's (1865-1936) aptly named 'Tiger, Tiger':

> **What of the hunting, hunter bold?**
> *Brother, the watch was long and cold.*
> **What of the quarry ye went to kill?**
> *Brother, he crops in the jungle still.*
> **Where is the power that made your pride?**
> *Brother, it ebbs from my flank and side.*
> **Where is the haste that ye hurry by?**
> *Brother, I go to my lair to die!*

I would like to pay tribute to each and every one of the Squadron's personnel for their energy, commitment and loyalty over the last 14 months. By any measure it was a challenging and turbulent time; our arrival at RAF Coningsby presented unfamiliar practices which were met with style and initiative; our immediate immersion in a full and sustained detachment programme brought both their enthusiasm and resilience to the fore; the prospect of operations was met with quiet resolve and efficient preparation; the uncertainty over our future tested their patience but they remained loyal and diligent; and, most recently, the need to disband in short order was met with determination and pride, despite obvious disappointment, and they performed magnificently to the very end. Throughout, it was their camaraderie and sense of humour that sustained the Squadron and I was struck, time and again, by their assured professionalism. It has been an immense privilege to work with them and their actions made my own task very much easier than it might have been. Jaguar Force Excellence will now become a memory, but the skills and experiences that its personnel have accrued will continue to make a contribution, directly to the RAF and elsewhere, long after the last Jaguar landed for the last time. My thoughts are with them all as we take separate paths.

6 Squadron will, I am sure, rise again. It is due to re-equip with the Typhoon and a new cadre will doubtless build their identity around the magnificent history of the Squadron. They will be the new Canopeners and I sincerely hope that they will be as proud as I have been to serve on 'Shiney Six'.

Karl Drage

Keith Chilton

Karl Drage